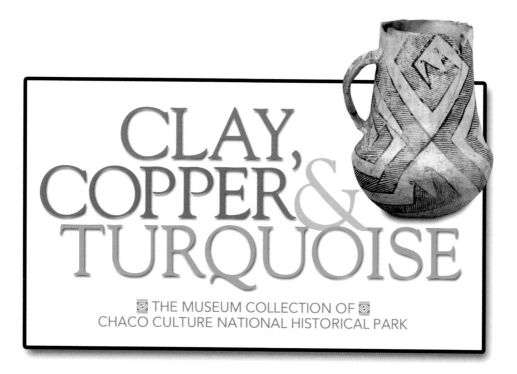

CLAY, COPPER & TURQUOISE

◈ THE MUSEUM COLLECTION OF ◈
CHACO CULTURE NATIONAL HISTORICAL PARK

WESTERN NATIONAL PARKS ASSOCIATION
TUCSON, ARIZONA

Ancient pottery and other artifacts give us valuable knowledge about the past. Federal, state, and local laws protect these artifacts and prohibit people from collecting them. Do not remove any sherds or other materials you may find and do not attempt to buy any ancient ceramics. You may be prosecuted, imprisoned, and fined up to $20,000.

Library of Congress Cataloging-in-Publication Data

Chaco Culture National Historical Park (N.M.)
  Clay, copper, and turquoise : the museum collection of Chaco Culture National Historical Park / [written by the National Park Service].
    p. cm.
  ISBN 1–58369–045–X
  1. Pueblo Indians—New Mexico—Chaco Culture National Historical Park—Antiquities. 2. Pueblo Indians—Material culture—New Mexico—Chaco Culture National Historical Park. 3. Pueblo Indians—Museums—New Mexico—Chaco Culture National Historical Park. 4. Ethnological museums and collections—New Mexico—Chaco Culture National Historical Park. 5. Chaco Culture National Historical Park (N.M.)—Antiquities. I. United States. National Park Service. II. Western National Parks Association. III. Title.
  E99.P9C465 2004
  978.9004'974'0074789—dc22
                                    2004003481

Written by National Park Service staff
Edited by Abby Mogollón
Designed by Dawn DeVries Sokol
Artifact photography by Khaled Bassim, Visual Information Specialist,
    National Park Service Museum Support Center
Photography by George H.H. Huey, front cover, JC Leacock pages 5 -7

Printing through Global Interprint
Printed in China

WESTERN NATIONAL PARKS ASSOCIATION

This book was inspired by a National Park Service Web project, initiated by the Museum Management program of the National Park Service. For more information, please visit: www.cr.nps.gov/museum/exhibits/chcu

CONTENTS

▨ OVERVIEW ▨

WHEN VISITORS WALK THROUGH CHACO CANYON, they marvel at the intricate masonry and the magnificent architecture, but something is missing in the quiet, empty rooms—the people themselves and their belongings. Some belongings are objects of extraordinary importance, others the common everyday stuff of living. They include finely handcrafted pots, delicately beaded necklaces, and durable and artful shoes. These personal items—the things the people created

Pueblo del Arroyo

with their hands for beauty, for survival, for pleasure—define the Chacoan world. These are the things that adorned people's bodies and filled their homes and their lives. These things help us to see the people and their culture as uniquely Chacoan.

People have called the Colorado Plateau of the Southwest home for at least ten thousand years. But from A.D. 850 to 1150, Chaco Canyon was a hub of ceremony, trade, and administration for the prehistoric Four Corners area—unlike anything before or since. During this extraordinary chapter in Puebloan history, people built small villages and monumental buildings, creating an urban ceremonial center. In the canyon people constructed spectacular public architecture, employing formal design, astronomical alignments, geometry, unique masonry, and engineering techniques that allowed enormous multistoried buildings.

These public and ceremonial buildings, constructed throughout the canyon, were massive masonry structures containing rooms, ceremonial rooms called "kivas," terraces, and plazas. The largest building—Pueblo Bonito—contained more than six hundred rooms and rose four, possibly five, stories high. Several hundred miles of formal roads radiated from the canyon and linked Chaco to other communities, both near and far.

The artistry and knowledge that pushed Chacoans to create the immense buildings so carefully also pushed them to make the things of everyday life carefully and artfully. The objects in this book represent the range of materials in the Chaco Collection housed at the University of New Mexico. They came from the daily lives of the Chacoan people—created by their hands. The Chacoan people fashioned the items with care, with skill, and with a sense of beauty. These objects help bring the past alive and paint a picture of a people living in an extraordinary land, in an extraordinary time.

Pueblo Bonito

THE CHACO COLLECTION

For more than a century, researchers excavated, studied, and surveyed in Chaco Canyon to understand the uniqueness of the Chacoan culture. From 1969 to 1985, the National Park Service conducted a multidisciplinary research program, known as the Chaco Project. Researchers identified more than 3,600 prehistoric and historic sites, establishing a comprehensive excavation program to investigate the entire span of human history in Chaco Canyon. During their excavations, researchers gathered artifacts such as ceramic vessels, stone projectile points, bone tools, construction beams, ornaments, fauna, soil, and pollen samples. Today, these artifacts form the core of the National Park Service's Chaco Collection.

Doorway, Pueblo Bonito

The Chaco Collection contains approximately one million artifacts from more than 120 sites in Chaco Canyon and the surrounding region. Because most of the artifacts were systematically collected and documented, the collection is extremely valuable for scientific studies. The archives in the Chaco Collection document more than one hundred years of excavation in Chaco Canyon and contain approximately 300 linear feet of records; 35,000 photographs; 7,000 color slides; 600 glass lantern slides; 2,000 maps; and 1,000 manuscripts.

After a century of research, an enormous body of knowledge about Chaco has been gained from archeology, architecture, ethnography, geology, history, physical anthropology, and, more recently, the oral history of the descendants of the people of Chaco. Many diverse clans and groups contributed to the cultural marvel centered in Chaco. Today, their descendants are members of many tribes in New Mexico and Arizona. The objects—everyday and exotic—made by the people of Chaco help tell part of a fascinating chapter in human history. The history and traditions of the modern-day Pueblos of New Mexico, the Hopi of Arizona, and the Navajo of the Four Corners region continue the narrative.

Pueblo del Arroyo

▨ DAILY LIFE ▨

Everyday objects used in Chaco Canyon one thousand years ago remind us of how similar people are through time. Like us, people then needed food and water containers, building and hunting tools, and clothing. They used fire starters to begin their cooking, awls and needles to make clothes and blankets, and cordage to hold or hang things. Gaming pieces enhanced leisure time.

Ceramic vessels were important objects in the everyday life of Chacoans. Ceramic use in the Southwest developed slowly. As people throughout the region became settled farmers, they built more permanent structures and increasingly used ceramics to enhance their daily activities.

The Chacoan people used pottery for food preparation, serving, and storage. Bowls, jars, canteens, seed jars, pitchers, and ladles came in a dazzling variety of shapes and sizes. The first pots were plain grayware. But early on, southwestern potters began decorating their pots

■ **PITCHER**
Chaco Black-on-White
A.D. 1075–1150
Clay. Height 18.7 cm, Diameter [max] 13.9 cm, Diameter [mouth] 9 cm

with black-painted geometric designs. Through time, these designs became elaborate and distinctive. At Chaco highly decorated whiteware and effigy vessels may have had special uses and meanings. Duck-shaped pots occur throughout the prehistoric Puebloan world. Chacoan potters also made miniatures of many vessel shapes.

Fragile items such as sandals, cordage, bone awls and needles, and wooden fire drills have survived more than one thousand years thanks to the arid southwestern climate. Most sandals, matting, and cordage in the collection were recovered from rock shelters (dry alcoves) that protected the items from rain and snow. Sandals and matting were woven from yucca and reeds. Cordage was made from yucca, cotton, human hair, sinew, and occasionally animal fur. Cordage was used to hang canteens and seed jars, to make sandal ties, and to haft tools. Rabbit fur and soft turkey feathers were twisted between plies of yucca cord to create fur and feather string—then intertwined to create fur and feather blankets.

The objects in this book all come from the Chaco Collection. They give us a tantalizing glimpse into the world of the men, women, and children of Chaco.

■ AWL
From Una Vida
A.D. 920–1120
Bone. Length 13.1 cm,
Width 1.2 cm,
Thickness 0.5 cm

■ NEEDLE
A.D. 975–1075
Bone. Length 15.6 cm,
Width 0.8 cm,
Thickness 0.3 cm

■ AWL
A.D. 1000–1200
Bone. Length 17 cm,
Width 1.1 cm,
Thickness 0.8 cm

■ NEEDLE
A.D. 1000–1050
Bone. Length 13.3 cm,
Width 1 cm, Thickness 0.8 cm

■ **AXE**
A.D. 1050–1100
Granite, with center grooves
for hafting. Length 21.1 cm,
Width 8.7 cm, Thickness 4.2 cm

■ **BOWL**
Gallup Black-on-White
From Pueblo Alto
A.D. 1030–1200
Clay. Height 17.4 cm, Diameter 38 cm

■ **CANTEEN**

From Una Vida

A.D. 1075–1300

Clay. Height 15.5 cm,

Diameter 17.6 cm

■ **CORDAGE**
From Gallo Cliff Dwelling
A.D. 1100–1200
Yucca fiber tied into a chain.
Length 11 cm, Width 3 cm,
Thickness 0.2 cm

FIRE STARTER KIT

■ FIRE DRILL HEARTH
From Gallo Cliff Dwelling
A.D. 1100–1200
Wood. Length 5.8 cm, Width 1.4 cm,
Thickness 1.2 cm

■ FIRE DRILL
From Gallo Cliff Dwelling
A.D. 1100–1200
Wood. Rounded end is blackened
from friction. Length 6.2 cm,
Diameter 1.1 cm

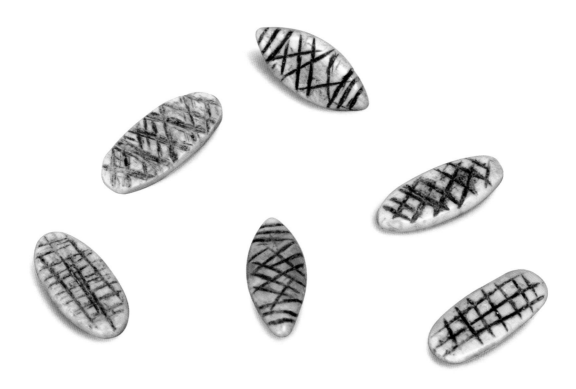

■ **GAMING PIECES**
A.D. 1000–1040
Incised bone. Length 1.7–1.9 cm,
Width 0.7–0.8 cm,
Thickness 0.2–0.3 cm

■ **JAR**
Exuberant Corrugated Grayware
A.D. 975–1050
Perforated holes below the rim were
used to hang this miniature jar. Clay.
Height 6.6 cm, Diameter 6.8 cm

■ **SANDAL**

A.D. 700–1200
Yucca, two-ply construction with
tie cords intact. Length 29 cm,
Width 13 cm, Thickness 2.8 cm

▧ SUBSISTENCE ▧

THE PEOPLE OF CHACO CANYON WERE FARMERS, HUNTERS, AND GATHERERS. They made full use of the diverse resources of their arid desert environment. In the early periods (Archaic through Basketmaker, from about 5500 B.C. to A.D. 700), hunting and gathering provided much of their food. Hunters needed sturdy spears and heavy projectile points to successfully hunt large game such as mule deer, mountain sheep, and elk. During this time, the people mounted projectile points on spears. Hunters used the atlatl, or spear thrower, to increase thrust and propel the spear forward.

About thirteen hundred years ago, with the start of the Pueblo Period, bows and arrows began to replace the atlatl. Projectile points diminished in size to fit the small reed arrow shafts. The smaller projectile points were suited to

CORN-GRINDING TOOLS

■ METATE
A.D. 920–1120
Lower trough slab for grinding corn into flour. Sandstone. Length 50 cm, Width 45 cm, Thickness 5.8 cm

■ MANO
A.D. 950–1030
Two-handed tool for grinding corn. Sandstone. Length 20.7 cm, Width 12.4 cm, Thickness 2.6 cm

■ CORN KERNELS
From Gallo Cliff Dwelling
A.D. 1100–1200
9.8 gms

hunting the small mammals and birds that were plentiful at Chaco. Hunters sought cottontail, jackrabbit, and prairie dog. Archeologists found a profusion of these creatures' bones in prehistoric middens (refuse areas) in Chaco Canyon. Changes in hunting gear correspond to changing animal populations, an increasingly sedentary village lifestyle, and population growth.

The Chaco Collection contains more than fifteen hundred points made from a wide variety of materials. These include petrified wood, chert, chalcedony, and obsidian. The Chaco Collection contains only a few fragments of historic-era Navajo-made arrows. However, in size and style they are similar to those found in prehistoric Puebloan sites.

Corn, beans, and squash dominated Chaco Canyon agriculture. Archeologists have uncovered corncobs from Chacoan times, which survived well because of the aridity in the Southwest. Remarkably, archeologists have also found piñon shells, squash seeds, and beans. To grow these crops, the Chacoans practiced dry farming, supplemented by irrigation and water control. Chacoans built canals, check dams, and ditches to take advantage of the water runoff during summer storms. They used digging sticks and stone hoes for planting. After the harvest, farmers stored seeds in jars, letting them dry over the winter. Dried corn kernels were ground into flour, using manos, hand-held round or oval grinding stones, and metates, large grinding slabs, often in a series of graduated coarseness. The archeological record shows that ancient Chacoans flourished in this semiarid landscape on a diverse and varied diet of plants and animals, both cultivated and wild.

■ ARROW

Puebloan or Navajo
Post A.D. 1540
Reed shaft and foreshaft, with
chalcedony projectile point hafted
with sinew.
Shaft. Length 13.5 cm, Diameter 0.6 cm
Point. Length 2.5 cm, Width 0.7 cm,
Thickness 0.4 cm

■ ATLATL (SPEAR THROWER)
FRAGMENT
Archaic Period
From Atlatl Cave, 2900–900 B.C.
A spear shaft was inserted into the grooved,
notched end of the atlatl. The atlatl provided
the hunter with a greatly increased range when
the spear was released. Wood. Length 16.4 cm,
Width 2.5 cm, Thickness 0.9 cm

■ DIGGING STICK
A.D. 1100–1200
Cottonwood with sinew cordage and
hide wrapping haft. Length 104 cm,
Diameter 3.8 cm

■ HOE (TCHAMAHIA)
A.D. 1000–1200
Basalt. Length 19.3 cm, Width 7.1 cm,
Thickness 2 cm

■ **HAFTED KNIFE BLADE**
A.D. 900–1100
Chert. Length 8.5 cm, Width 4 cm,
Thickness 0.8 cm

SEEDS AND KERNELS

■ **SQUASH SEEDS**
From Gallo Cliff Dwelling
A.D. 1100–1200

■ **PIÑON SHELLS**
From Gallo Cliff Dwelling
A.D. 1100–1200

■ **CORN KERNELS**
From Gallo Cliff Dwelling
A.D. 1100–1200

■ **WATERMELON SEED**
From Gallo Cliff Dwelling
A.D. 1100–1200

■ **SEED JAR**
Black Mesa Black-on-White
A.D. 1000–1200
Used to store seeds over the winter.
Clay. Height 12 cm, Diameter 19.3 cm

CRAFTSMANSHIP

MANY CHACOANS WERE MASTER ARTISANS. THEY LEFT HUGE QUANTITIES of utilitarian and decorated ceramics, delicately carved pendants, beadwork, and refined stone artifacts such as projectile points. Archeologists have found workshop remains in small villages and in the great buildings at Chaco.

Ornament making involved obtaining the raw material locally or through trade, perhaps by quarrying it, and then shaping, grinding, drilling, and polishing. Artisans made beads, many less than two millimeters in diameter, from turquoise, bone, shell, shale, and argillite. From these materials they created pendants, which were also carved from gypsum, selenite, and schist.

Chacoans sculpted animal effigies in clay, or carved them from turquoise, jet, argillite, and wood. Archeologists have found depictions of animals such as antelope, badgers, birds, deer, dogs, ducks, frogs, and snakes. Some effigies are highly stylized, but many bird and frog figures are easily identifiable.

People shaped and polished beads by abrading raw materials against sandstone lapidary stones. The

■ BEADS
A.D. 615–650
Bone.
Length 1.6-3.4 cm,
Diameter .45-4 cm

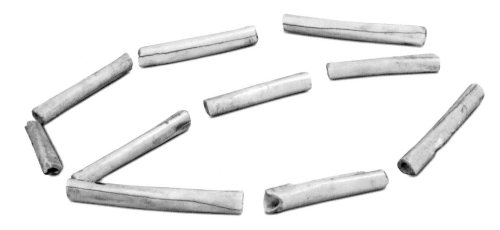

26

extraordinary smoothness of these abraders indicates heavy use over a long period of time. Chacoans may have used cactus spines or porcupine quills to make holes in beads and pendants; the small stone drills found so far are too coarse to have made the tiny perforations. Artisans also carefully shaped turquoise and argillite into small squares and used them as mosaic inlay on vessels, bone tools, and effigies. The quantity of beads produced is staggering: In a burial at Pueblo Bonito, archeologists found more than fifteen thousand turquoise beads and pendants.

The Chacoan people valued color, and they adorned themselves with turquoise jewelry, brilliant macaw feathers, and shells. Using stone mortars, they ground minerals such as hematite (red), limonite (yellow), azurite (blue), malachite (green), and gypsum (white) into pigments for paints. Mixing the pigments with water or vegetal oils created paints for decorating objects, including arrows and other wooden items. Chacoans also used pigments to paint murals on plastered walls and to paint pictographs (painted symbols and images) on the sandstone canyon walls.

Today, Pueblo artists maintain the artistic achievements of the Chacoan people. Turquoise mosaic jewelry, minute shell beadwork, carved stone animal figurines, and intricately painted pottery continue to enrich our world and reveal the enduring legacy of the Chacoan people and their descendants.

■ **BEADS**
From Una Vida
A.D. 920–1120
Shale.
Diameter .18-.28,
Thickness 0.1-.15 cm

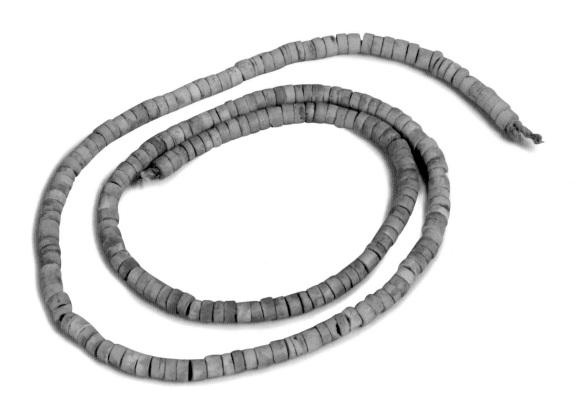

■ **BEAD NECKLACE**
[restrung]
A.D. 1000–1200
Argillite. Average bead
Diameter 0.3 cm

■ **EFFIGY VESSEL**
Puerco Black-on-White
A.D. 1030–1200
Clay. Height 6.4 cm, Length 8.4 cm,
Width 4.7 cm

■ **FETISH**

From Una Vida

A.D. 920–1120

A fetish, often a carved animal, is believed to have magical power to protect or help its owner.

Jet. Length 3.9 cm, Width 1.2 cm, Thickness 1.1 cm

■ INLAY PIECES
From Pueblo Alto
A.D. 1020–1140
Turquoise. Length 0.23 cm;
Width 0.22 cm, Thickness 0.11 cm
Argillite. Length 0.96 cm,
Width 0.38 cm, Thickness 0.12 cm

PAINT TOOL KIT

■ **PAINT CYLINDER**
A.D. 700–1200
Hematite. Length 9.1 cm,
Width 2.4 cm, Thickness 0.8 cm

■ **MORTAR**
A.D. 900–1150
Sandstone. Length 11.1 cm,
Width 8 cm, Thickness 2.3 cm

■ **PENDANT**
From Pueblo Bonito
A.D. 1020–1150
The bird effigy pendant had a drilled
base and the wings may have been
inlaid. Hematite. Length 2.5 cm,
Width 1.0 cm, Thickness 1.0 cm

■ **PENDANT**

A.D. 1000–1200

Turquoise. Length 2 cm,
Width 1.8 cm, Thickness 0.2 cm

■ **VESSEL FRAGMENT**
[animal effigy]
A.D. 1000–1200
Clay. Length 9.7 cm, Width 6.2 cm,
Height 6.5 cm

▤ TRADE ▤

TODAY, CHACO CANYON LACKS THE BASIC RESOURCES FOR LIVING. One thousand years ago, the situation was not very different. As it does today, the Chaco Wash ran only seasonally. Agriculture in the canyon—and on much of the Colorado Plateau—was risky. As a result, the Chacoans engaged in regional and long-distance trade.

Corn and utilitarian goods were imported into Chaco from close by. Pottery came from the San Juan region to the north, the Chuska Mountains to the west, and the Zuni area to the south. Potters produced very few pots in Chaco Canyon, probably because the demand for wood to construct the great houses and heat homes depleted fuel sources needed to fire ceramics.

High-quality cherts—used for stone tools such as projectile points, knives, and scrapers—came from the nearby areas. These include Brushy Basin chert from the northwestern San Juan Basin, Narbona Pass chert from the Chuska Mountains, and Zuni spotted chert from the Zuni Mountains.

Chacoans also imported obsidian, a volcanic glass. The nearest sources of obsidian are the Jemez Mountain range to the east of Chaco and Mt. Taylor to the south. Obsidian was widely used because it could be flaked to produce knives and blades with extremely sharp edges. Local trade also allowed people to share information, such as where to find abundant game, reliable springs, good piñon nut crops,

■ **VESSEL HANDLE**
From Pueblo Alto/East Ruin
A.D. 1020–1140
The underbelly of the frog has perforation for hanging.
Clay. Length 4.9 cm,
Width 4.3 cm,
Thickness 1.6 cm

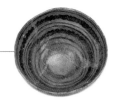

or areas where the rains were falling. This kind of communication was crucial to people living in a marginal environment such as the arid Southwest.

The people of Chaco Canyon also traded for non-utilitarian items, sometimes called "exotic goods." Turquoise was imported from more than one hundred miles away and used as decorative mosaic inlay or made into ornaments such as pendants, earrings, and beads. Workshops were common in Chaco. Some archeologists speculate that turquoise ornament production helped make Chaco Canyon a regional trading center. Other goods came from even farther away. Long-distance trade brought macaws, shells, and copper bells into Chaco Canyon from Mexico. The people shaped shells from the Pacific Ocean and the Gulf of California into a variety of ornaments, such as pendants, beads, and bracelets. They fashioned conch shells into trumpets. The Chacoans valued macaws for their feathers and kept them in captivity in Pueblo Bonito. Long-distance trade routes were well established and long-lived. Puebloan trading expeditions to Sonora and the Gulf of California continued well into the mid-1800s. Today, throughout the modern Pueblo world, artisans and jewelry makers use shell and turquoise to continue the artistic forms and traditions that began in Chaco.

■ **VESSEL**
Red Mesa Black-on-White
A.D. 875–1040
Clay. Height 8.0 cm,
Diameter 14 cm

■ **BEADS**
A.D. 1050–1100
Turquoise. Diameter 0.35–0.5 cm,
Thickness 0.2–0.3 cm

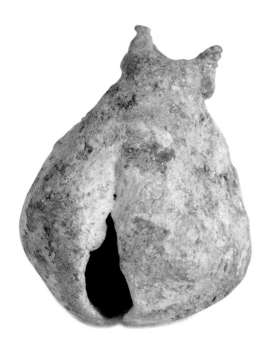

■ **BELL WITH TINKLER**
From Pueblo Alto
A.D. 1020–1140
The loop was molded separately from
the body and later fused to it. The tinkler
was made of either stone or clay. Trade
good from northern Mexico.
Copper. Length 1.2 cm, Diameter 0.9 cm

■ BOWL
Abajo Black-on-Orange
A.D. 900–1100
Trade ware from the
northern San Juan region.
Clay. Height 8.6 cm, Diameter 18.1 cm

■ BRACELET
A.D. 1050–1100
Shell from the Gulf of California
Glycymeris gigantean shell. Diameter
6.9 cm, Thickness 0.5 cm

■ LADLE

Chuskan Whiteware
From Pueblo Alto
A.D. 1020–1140
Trade ware from the Chuska region
west of Chaco Canyon.
Clay. Length 24.1 cm, Width 11.8 cm,
Height 6.5 cm

■ **MUG**
Mesa Verde Black-on-White
A.D. 1200–1300
Trade ware from the Mesa Verde
region to the north.
Clay. Height 9 cm, Diameter 11.2 cm

■ **OLLA**
Red Mesa Black-on-White
A.D. 875–1040
Clay. Height 26.1 cm,
Diameter 24.5 cm, Mouth 7.9 cm

■ PENDANT
A.D. 775–1100
Shell from the Gulf of California.
Argopecten circularis, or Schoolhouse
Mesa Shell. Length 2 cm,
Width 0.9 cm, Thickness 0.3 cm

■ **PENDANT**

A.D. 1000–1200

There were workshops for bead manufacture and ornamentation at Chaco. It is unclear whether this incised shell pendant was made at Chaco or if it was made in Baja California and then traded to Chaco.

Glycymeris gigantean shell. Length 3.4 cm, Width 0.7 cm, Thickness 0.4 cm

■ **PROJECTILE POINT**
Archaic, possibly reworked Paleo-Indian
c. 6000–1000 B.C.
Obsidian, with oblique pressure
flaking. Length 4.9 cm, Width 2 cm,
Thickness 0.5 cm

FURTHER READING

Frazier, Kendrick, *People of Chaco*. New York: W.W. Norton & Company, 1999.

Lister, Robert, and Florence Lister, *Chaco Canon, Archaeology and Archaeologists*. Albuquerque, New Mexico: University of New Mexico Press, 1999.

Noble, David Grant *New Light on Chaco*. Santa Fe, New Mexico: School of American Research Press, 1984.

Stuart, David, *Anasazi America*. Albuquerque, New Mexico: University of New Mexico Press, 2001.

Vivian, R. Gwinn, and Bruce Hilpert, *The Chaco Handbook*. Salt Lake City: University of Utah Press, 2002.